North American Indians Today

North American Indians Today

Apache

Cherokee

Cheyenne

Comanche

Creek

Crow

Huron

Iroquois

Navajo

Ojibwa

Osage

Potawatomi

Pueblo

Seminole

Sioux

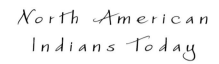

North American Indians Today

Ojibwa

by
George L. Cornell
and
Gordon Henry Jr.

Mason Crest Publishers

Philadelphia

Mason Crest Publishers Inc.
370 Reed Road
Broomall, Pennsylvania 19008
(866) MCP-BOOK (toll free)

First printing
1 2 3 4 5 6 7 8 9 10
Library of Congress Cataloging-in-Publication Data on file at the Library of Congress.
ISBN: 1-59084-673-7
1-59084-663-X (series)

Design by Lori Holland.
Composition by Bytheway Publishing Services, Binghamton, New York.
Cover design by Benjamin Stewart.
Printed and bound in the Hashemite Kingdom of Jordan.

Photography by Benjamin Stewart. Picture on p. 6 by Keith Rosco. Photos on pp. 18,
50, 56 courtesy of Viola Ruelke Gommer; pp. 60, 65 courtesy of the Elijah Elk Cultural
Center.

Contents

Why is it so important that Indians be brought into the "mainstream" of American life?
I would not know how to interpret this phrase to my people.
The closest I would be able to come would be "a big wide river".
Am I then to tell my people that they are to be thrown into the big, wide river of the United States?

Earl Old Person
Blackfeet Tribal Chairman

Introduction

In the midst of twenty-first-century North America, how do the very first North Americans hold on to their unique cultural identity? At the same time, how do they adjust to the real demands of the modern world? Earl Old Person's quote on the opposite page expresses the difficulty of achieving this balance. Even the common values of the rest of North America—like fitting into the "mainstream"—may seem strange or undesireable to North American Indians. How can these groups of people thrive and prosper in the twenty-first century without losing their traditions, the ways of thinking and living that have been handed down to them by their ancestors? How can they keep from drowning in North America's "big, wide river"?

Thoughts from the Series Consultant

Each of the books in this series was written with the help of Native scholars and tribal leaders from the particular tribe. Based on oral histories as well as written documents, these books describe the current strategies of each Native nation to develop its economy while maintaining strong ties with its culture. As a result, you may find that these books read far differently from other books about Native Americans.

Over the past centuries, Native groups have faced increasing pressure to conform to the wishes of the governments that took their lands. Often brutally inhumane methods were implemented to change Native social systems. These books describe the ways that Native groups refused to be passive recipients of change, even in the face of these past atrocities. Heroic individuals worked to fit external changes into local conditions. This struggle continues today.

The legacy of the past still haunts the psyche of both Native and non-Native people of North America; hopefully, these books will help correct some misunderstandings. And even with the difficulties encountered by past and current Native leaders, Native nations continue to thrive. As this series illustrates, Native populations continue to increase—and they have clearly persevered against incredible odds. North American culture's big, wide river may be deep and cold—but Native Americans are good swimmers!

—*Martha McCollough*

Breaking Stereotypes

One way that some North Americans may "drown" Native culture is by using stereotypes to think about North American Indians. When we use stereotypes to think about a group of people, we assume things about them because of their race or cultural group. Instead of taking time to understand individual differences and situations, we lump together everyone in a certain group. In reality, though, every person is different. More than two million Native people live in North America, and they are as *diverse* as any other group. Each one is unique.

Even if we try hard to avoid stereotypes, however, it isn't always easy to know what words to use. Should we call the people who are native to North America Native Americans—or American Indians—or just Indians?

The word "Indian" probably comes from a mistake—when Christopher Columbus arrived in the New World, he thought he had reached India, so he called the people he found there Indians. Some people feel it doesn't make much sense to call Native Americans "Indians." (Suppose Columbus had thought he landed in China instead of India; would we today call Native people "Chinese"?) Other scholars disagree; for example, Russell Means, Native politician and activist, claims that the word "Indian" comes from Columbus saying the native people were *en Dios*—"in God," or naturally spiritual.

Many Canadians use the term "First Nations" to refer to the Native peoples who live there, and people in the United States usually speak of Native Americans. Most Native people we talked to while we were writing these books prefer the simple term "Indian"—or they would rather use the names of their tribes. (We have used the term "North American Indians" for our series to distinguish this group of people from the inhabitants of India.)

Even the definition of what makes a person "Indian" varies. The U.S. government recognizes certain groups as tribal nations (almost 500 in all). Each nation then decides how it will enroll people as members of that tribe. Tribes may require a particular amount of Indian blood, tribal membership of the father or the mother, or other *criteria*. Some enrolled tribal members who are legally "Indian" may not look Native at all; many have blond hair and blue eyes and others have clearly African features. At the same time, there are thousands of Native people whose tribes have not yet been officially recognized by the government.

We have done our best to write books that are as free from stereotypes as possible. But you as the reader also play a part. After reading one of these books, we hope you won't think: "The Cheyenne are all like this" or "Iroquois are all like that." Each person in this world is unique, whatever their culture. Stereotypes shut people's minds—but these books are intended to open your mind. North American Indians today have much wisdom and beauty to offer.

Some people consider American Indians to be a historical topic only, but Indians today are living, contributing members of North American society. The contributions of the various Indian cultures enrich our world—and North America would be a very different place without the Native people who live there. May they never be lost in North America's "big, wide river"!

An Ojibwa artist's interpretation of the great Eagle that came to their aid in a time of great suffering.

Chapter 1

Oral Traditions

Aanii!
("Hello" in the Ojibwa/Chippewa language.)

For cultures to continue, for people to survive, certain people will make sacrifices. In the Christian religion, for example, Jesus sacrificed his life so that people could renew their relationship with God. As a young man, Buddha left the safety and security of his home so he could find out the truth about human suffering—and from his sacrifice, his continual meditation on human suffering, Buddhism was born. Among the Ojibwa/Chippewa people there are also many *adisokan* (stories) about men and women who were willing to sacrifice so that the people could survive. Francis Cree, a Turtle Mountain Ojibwa who is also known as Eagleheart, tells one such story.

A long time ago there was great suffering among the *Anishinabe*, the people. They were starving, and an **epidemic** was sweeping throughout the camp. In those days, when there wasn't enough food to go around, when hardships were at their worst, some of the old people would choose to die rather than burden the people.

One old man who had chosen this option said, "I've lived a good life. I've lived a long time and I would like what little we have to go to the children and to those who need help." So this old man went off into the woods by himself to die.

He wandered around looking for a place to die. After a while he came to a great and beautiful tree. When he saw it, he said to himself, "This is the place. This is where I will die." He lay down under the tree, waiting to die.

After some time he heard a voice. "You. What are you doing?"

The old man sat up. He looked around in all directions, but he saw nothing. So he lay back down.

The sacred traditions of the Anishinabe have been passed down for many generations by word of mouth. Tom Peters (Niigaanakwat) of the Grand Traverse Band is a traditional storyteller. He is also the Cultural Division Director for the Sault St. Marie Tribe of Chippewa Indians.

The Eagle showed the old man how to build a sacred nest, the sweat lodge.
These wigwams at the Elijah Elk Cultural Center in Mt. Pleasant, Michigan, are
similar to those used for sweats.

Soon the voice called out again. "You under the tree, what are you doing down there?"

This time the old man looked up. At the top of the tree he saw a giant eagle. So he said to the eagle, "I'm an old man. My people are sick and starving, and I can't do anything for them. Rather than be a burden to my people, I've come here to die."

"You don't have to do that," the eagle answered. "I have something for you, something you can bring back to the people." In the top branches of the tree was a great nest, and the eagle took his talons and pushed the nest out of the tree. As the nest floated down, it turned over and over until it landed upside down on the earth.

"I'm going to teach you all about this nest," the eagle said, and he pro-

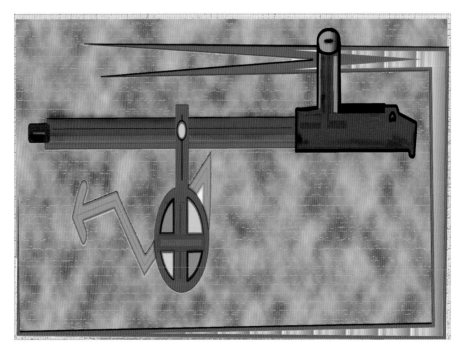

The pwaagun *or peace pipe was given to the Anishinabe to resolve conflict, maintain goodwill, and pray to the Creator for assistance. This painting by Ojibwa artist Turtle Heart is titled* The Family Pipe.

ceeded to give the old man instructions. He told the old man to make a fire to the east of the nest, and then he told him to heat stones in that fire. He also told the old man to cover the nest with bark and animal skins and make an eastern doorway in the nest. He wanted the old man to bring the rest of his people to sit in a circle around the inside of the nest. Then he told the old man to bring the hot stones and put them in the center of the nest, in a small circular pit in the earth.

"You'll need something to move those hot stones in there," the eagle said, "so you get two sticks to move the stones. Those sticks will remind you of my legs, the same legs that pushed this nest down to earth for you. When the people and the stones are inside there, you must also bring in a bucket of water.

"Make a tail," the eagle continued, "out of the leaves of a tree, and use that tail to dip into the bucket, so you can shake water over the hot stones to make steam. That tail will remind you of my tail. That steam will remind you of the clouds I fly in, and it will help to cleanse and purify you as you and the people pray inside the nest.

"This is a spiritual nest," the eagle finished. "A *manido wadiswan*. It will bring blessing and healing to the people. It will help you in times of hardship. Through it you will remember to give thanks, to be thankful for all the gifts of creation."

The old man went back and told the people in the camp about the nest. To this day many Ojibwa/Chippewa people still use the sweat lodge, the spiritual nest, for physical and spiritual healing and to give thanks.

The story Francis Cree tells about the spiritual nest is just one story among a great many stories in the oral tradition of the Ojibwa/Chippewa people. There are stories about journeys. There are stories about how the world was made and about how things came to be part of the Ojibwa/Chippewa culture. Some stories explain where the people came from, while others give prophecies that foretell possibilities for the future. Stories explain the origins of ceremonies and the origin of the seasons; other stories tell about the giving of names. Ojibwa/Chippewa stories may establish a relationship between humans and animals, and they may tell of animal behavior. Other stories explain human beings' responsibilities to the earth and family. Still other stories tell of ghosts, the afterlife, and our relationship to the stars. And some stories tell about giants, little people, and water spirits.

For the Ojibwa/Chippewa people, these *adisokan* served as teaching models, as entertainment, and as reminders of our connection to our ancestors and our relatives. The stories had—and still have—the capacity to teach people about human emotions and about human behavior. They often include practical knowledge about how to make or do things. But more than that, stories helped the people survive.

Ojibwa/Chippewa stories also tell of heroes and heroines, like Anishinabe (the first man), Sky Woman, and Nanaboozhoo (also known as Winaboozhoo and Nanapush). Nanaboozhoo may be the most constant character in these stories; he is the trickster, part spirit, part human, and hundreds of stories tell about him.

In one story about Nanaboozhoo we learn

> Some Ojibwa/Chippewa elders say that a long time ago stories were only told in winter, and to this day some storytellers will only tell stories if there is snow on the ground.

This painting by Ojibwa artist Turtle Heart is titled Seven Songs in Time. *He explains its meaning: "Here are the seven teachers of Ojibwa history. These teachers brought us the knowledge of the seven fires, teachings that are at the heart of Ojibwa culture. Through the ceremonial teachings, the Ojibwa have developed a great understanding of the human spirit and its journey on this earth."*

how he took a long journey to find his father, Epingishmook. When he found his father, he ended up fighting with him. After the battle, his father gave him the sacred *pwaagun*, the peace pipe, to bring back to the people to help resolve conflict, to maintain goodwill, and to use for prayer to the Creator.

Another story tells of how Nanaboozhoo defeated a giant by going inside the giant and spearing his heart. In these stories, Nanaboozhoo displays a wide range of attributes and abilities in a wide variety of contexts. Nanaboozhoo can transform himself into animals; he speaks the languages of birds and other animals; he may show great intelligence and generosity in one story and show ignorance, greed, lust, jealousy, or competitiveness in other stories.

Other stories recount the migrations of the Ojibwa/Chippewa people.

This great body of stories tells how the original *dodems*, or clans, migrated from the great water in the east to the west where the "food grows on the water." The migration stories also tell us that along the way, the people stopped and settled in various places, wherever they beheld a vision of the sacred megis shell above the horizon. Some of these migration stories are laid out in **pictographs** on scrolls made from birch bark.

"Ojibwa" and "Chippewa" are two names for the same tribe. Some people prefer one, and some the other, but both mean the same group of people. Many from this tribe call themselves the *Anishinabe*, which in their own language means simply "the People."

Many of these migration scrolls are part of the teachings of Midewiwin Society of the Anishinabe. The *midewiwin* are one of the oldest, most respected spiritual associations in North America. Through ceremonies and seasonal teaching lodges, the midewiwin have helped the Ojibwa/Chippewa people to remember traditions, to learn the use of medicines, to heal, to share spiritual gifts, and to live a good life according to their cultural heritage.

Songs are also an important part of Ojibwa/Chippewa oral tradition. Just as there are a variety of stories, there are also a variety of songs for a variety of purposes and occasions. The Ojibwa/Chippewa people sing morning songs, death songs, dream songs, healing songs, ceremonial songs, animal songs, honoring songs, gathering songs, naming songs, charm songs, personal songs, social songs, and protection songs.

Many of the stories from this oral tradition are also part of "the teachings of the seven fires," or the seven fires prophecies of the Anishinabe (the Ojibwa/Chippewa people). According to the teachings, seven prophets came to the people. At that time, the Ojibwa/Chippewa people were living a good life of abundance and peace on the northeastern shore of North America. Each of the seven prophets told a story of a specific era of the future. These stories predicted the hardships and challenges of the years to come, just as they told of what the people would become through the choices they would make. For example, the seven fires teachings tell how generations of the Ojibwa/Chippewa people would one day lose their traditions and stories, only to have a later generation find them again.

Today, people have returned to Anishinabe spiritual traditions, and the stories are being told again, with greater frequency to a wide variety of people. Many contemporary Ojibwa/Chippewa believe that the new generation predicted by the seven fires prophecy is living now.

Powwows are one way North American Indians are celebrating their cultures. This young man in traditional clothes is at the powwow on the National Mall in Washington, D.C., summer of 2002.

Chapter 2

History

"If you do not move, you will be destroyed," proclaimed an Anishinabe prophet. According to tradition, the people heeded his words, which may have been warning of the Europeans' arrival. They left their homes by what is today known as the Atlantic Ocean and embarked on an *epic* journey westward to a promised new homeland, "where food grows on water." The Anishinabe, who have become known in the contemporary period as the Ojibwa or Chippewa, thus migrated into the Upper Great Lakes region sometime before contact with European *colonial* governments.

This migration took many years and was very difficult for the people. The Anishinabe migrated from a woodland/coastal environment to a very similar environment in the Upper Great Lakes region, into what are today the states of Michigan, Wisconsin, Minnesota, and North Dakota and the Canadian provinces of Ontario, Manitoba, and Saskatchewan.

The Ojibwa/Chippewa have always been one of the largest tribal groups in North America. Not only do they represent one of the largest populations, but their tribal network and villages may have controlled more territory than any other tribe.

Bud Byron shares the traditional ways of the Anishinabe with visitors at Sugar Island Culture Camp in Sault St. Marie, Michigan. Today's Ojibwa/Chippewa people keep their unique cultural beliefs and practices alive in the modern world.

The Ojibwa/Chippewa relied on hunting, fishing, gardening, and gathering natural foods to live. Their environment had a great number of mammals and fish; deer, elk, caribou, moose, bear, rabbits, and other animals were their primary protein source, along with whitefish, trout, bass, pike, walleye, and sturgeon. In addition to these foods, the Ojibwa harvested wild rice and collected nuts and berries as well as planted seasonal gardens.

The Ojibwa/Chippewa possessed the technology to harvest animals and fish efficiently. They used bows and arrows, but mostly they relied on traps and snares for mammals, while netting and spearing fish. They also constructed fish weirs (large traps) to catch fish. The Ojibwa ate well and enjoyed good health in the areas where they lived.

Life was not easy since there was a great deal of physical work to be done, but all in all, life was good. The people made baskets and boats from birch bark, and they could boil their foods in waterproof containers by using red-hot stones. Again, the land provided for the needs of the people, and the Ojibwa were adept at providing for their immediate families and extended families (clans).

The rise of European colonial governments in North America during the sixteenth century, however, had a serious impact on Ojibwa life. The Europeans introduced diseases to North America that killed large numbers of Native people because they lacked *immunity* to the new germs. The rise of the fur trade also had an impact on Native people; they started to trap fur-bearing mammals and traded the hides for European goods. Trade with the Europeans became critically important so that tribes could maintain a balance of power between themselves. European colonies had a technological

This map shows the location of the Ojibwa/Chippewa, along with other tribes, when Europeans arrived in the Great Lakes area.

advantage. Trading for rifles, gunpowder, and lead became important activities in maintaining the balance of power.

The Ojibwa also had to deal with competition between colonial interests. They allied themselves with New France, thereby *alienating* the British who were active in setting up successful colonies in the East. During the seventeenth, eighteenth, and nineteenth centuries, the Ojibwa were engaged in wars of *empire* between colonial and national governments. When France was defeated as a power in North America, the Ojibwa allied with the British against the pressure of the freedom-seeking American colonies' interests and forces in their territories. Eventually, however, the British were defeated, and Indian policy was left completely in the hands of the new American federal government.

Indian treaties became an important vehicle for the new government's dealings with the Ojibwa/Chippewa. These treaties were authorized by the Supremacy Clause of the U.S. Constitution as one form of the "supreme law of the land." Federal law also determined that the U.S. Congress would

The Ojibwa/Chippewa people moved from their ancient homes on the Eastern Coast to live in the Upper Great Lakes area of the Midwest. There, the forest environment provided abundant game, fish, and wild foods.

In historic times, the Anishinabe lived in wigwams made of wooden frames covered with bark. This wigwam framework is outside of the Bahweting Anishinabe Public School Academy, in Sault St. Marie, Michigan.

have plenary (absolute) power over Indian affairs. The laws and acts that were passed would have a deep impact on Indian life.

The Ojibwa and other tribal groups had little input into the decisions being made by the U.S. Congress that would affect their lives. The government treated Indians as if they were children. Congress passed law after law that continued to make Indians poor in their own land. The treaties that were signed also resulted in the Ojibwa having less and less access to the resources that their life had depended on. Numerous treaties were signed in both the United States and Canada giving more and more Ojibwa land to these countries.

Through these treaties and land **cessions**, the United States and Canada, and their respective states and provinces, gained access to millions of acres of timber, mining resources, and fresh water resources like the commercial fishery in the Great Lakes. These resources, gained through treaties, provided the economic base for non-Indian citizens who were taking possession of the land. Federal governments sold much of the Indian land acquired through treaties with the Ojibwa/Chippewa to local citizens, and the sale of the land helped to fund government. Unfortunately, the continued loss of land for the Ojibwa resulted in impoverished communities at the turn of the twentieth century.

A great deal of **discrimination** was leveled at Indian citizens during these

The tribal flag of the Sault St. Marie tribe of Chippewa Indians incorporates numerous elements of their heritage. The round shape is that of a medicine wheel. The crane in the center symbolizes the eloquence of leadership. The turtle in the center represents Mother Earth. The mountain ash tree, which survives where other trees cannot, represents endurance of the people and culture. The four directions, animals, and colors each have spiritual significance.

years. Most Indians did not become citizens of the United States until the General Indian Citizenship Act was passed in 1924. Educational opportunities were also extremely limited, and few Ojibwa people had access to higher education. In the late 1800s and early 1900s, most Ojibwa communities lived in poverty and were seriously undereducated in comparison to most other Americans.

These conditions persisted, even though the United States and Canada had an official duty to oversee and assist these native populations under the terms of treaties and federal agreements. This situation didn't begin to change for the Ojibwa/Chippewa until the years immediately following World War II.

During the war years, Ojibwa who were not serving in the armed forces of the United States or Canada found work in the **war industries**. In many instances, "Rosie the Riveter," the famous female war industry worker, was an Ojibwa woman building airplanes. When the war was over in 1945, many Ojibwa families stayed in cities where work was plentiful.

In the post-war years, Indians across the nation began to demand fair treatment from the government. Rights that were guaranteed under various treaties were reaffirmed through cases won in federal courts. Both Canada and the United States were pressured to honor their promises to Native people. During this period, the Ojibwa, like many other Indian groups, experienced incredible growth in the complexity of tribal governments and economic activities. Since the late 1960s, a true renewal of Ojibwa culture and language has also taken place.

The concept of "self-determination" began to take hold in Indian Country. This idea holds that Native people have the right to play a key role in determining policy that will affect their lives. In other words, the Ojibwa/Chippewa began to take themselves and their governments very seriously. Tribal **sovereignty** also became a hot topic, and Ojibwa governments

In winter, the powwow grounds in Sault St. Marie are quiet under a blanket of snow. When spring comes, however, the Ojibwa will celebrate their culture here with dances and contests.

Chippewa casinos, such as Kewadin Casino in Sault St. Marie, Michigan, have been built across the Great Lakes and Upper Midwest regions.

demanded "government-to-government" relations. They began to deal directly with federal and state governments and to play important roles in determining regional and national policy on Indian affairs. This fact, coupled with the economic changes that have occurred on Ojibwa reservations, helped to begin the rebuilding of Ojibwa communities during recent years.

Ojibwa/Chippewa casinos now dot the landscape in the Great Lakes and Upper Midwest. These tribal enterprises, operated under federal regulation, provide much needed economic support for tribal agendas and initiatives. Chippewa tribes are supporting numerous community services and activities through gaming revenues. The tribes have created jobs for tribal members and thousands of non-Indian workers, and they have also created higher education scholarships for tribal members. Some communities even have tribal colleges.

Without question, many changes have occurred in Indian Country since the Europeans began to establish colonies in North America. Throughout it all, the Anishinabe have persisted and adapted. They still retain elements of their distinct culture, and they have preserved their *reservations*.

The Ojibwa/Chippewa are on the threshold of new and important changes once again. Today, they are charged with creating a future for their membership that will recapture some of the past. Ojibwa tribal governments are working to acquire larger land bases and to provide additional services to ensure a bright future. Tribes are supporting the training of lawyers and professionals so as to protect tribal interests as they move into the future.

The future being created by the Ojibwa/Chippewa is closely tied to the old teachings. The sons and daughters of a once great nation are working to reestablish the Ojibwa heritage and voice in North America. Some of the greatest Anishinabe history is yet to be written. It will be forged in the years ahead as Ojibwa/Chippewa governments grow and prosper. They will create new opportunities and *paradigms* for tribal life and members.

The Saginaw Chippewa tribal seal.

Chapter 3

Current Government

In 2001, *Lake Superior Magazine* named their Achievement Award winner for the year—the Grand Portage Band of Lake Superior Chippewa. The magazine commented that "Today, all First Nations of the lake deserve praise for getting their people's needs heard and met." It went on to note: "Their efforts help everyone. Many are replenishing natural resources, stocking fish or plants. Tribal businesses, like casinos, benefit extended communities and create job opportunities." The successes of modern Ojibwa/Chippewa Indians are due, in large part, to the efforts of their tribal governments.

The current governments of most Ojibwa/Chippewa tribes are very similar to city, provincial, and state governments as well as the U.S. federal government. They are based on **democratic process**, **direct representation**, and individual voting rights. The present systems, however, are very different from the way in which tribal affairs were conducted in the past.

Historically, villages were organized along clan lines (extended families), and leadership positions were held by people who had demonstrated

Tribal newspapers enable members to stay updated on the politics, opportunities, and other happenings in their community. Brenda Austin is proud to work for the Sault Tribe News.

their abilities as civil leaders or leaders in times of conflict. People were born into the clan of their father and were prohibited from marrying another member of the same clan. These marriages between clans formed the basis of community life, since it extended the number of relatives a person had. Leadership was specialized into various categories (such as medicine, **oratory**, and spiritual matters) and **vested** in people who had demonstrated over time their concern for their neighbors. Most leadership consisted of elders who had vast experience in the matters of village life and decision making. No one was "elected" to any post; people in the village entrusted these tasks to people they respected. The community had watched people function in these roles for years, so they knew a person's strengths and weaknesses.

No single person in any of the leadership positions in the village had the power to tell another person what to do. This is a major difference between many governments and the historic way in which Ojibwa tribes managed their affairs. The villages were completely independent to make decisions in their best interest, and they often did not agree on a course of action. That was acceptable to the Ojibwa/Chippewa people, but not always acceptable to **Western** governments that believed in **centralized** power.

The Ojibwa/Chippewa villages' ways of doing things (their governance) was not centralized and placed great emphasis on the rights of individuals. As more and more Chippewa villages and groups signed treaties with the U.S. federal government, it became important to the United States that tribal governments mimic the workings of the federal government. Through treaties, the United States began to relate to the Chippewa villages as a larger **collective**, when in reality none ever existed. The Anishinabe were a collection of people who shared a language, culture, and clans, but they fiercely retained their individuality and authority to govern their own affairs. Of course, this loose structure proved difficult for the federal govern-

Tribal office buildings, such as that of the Sault tribe, handle innumerable tribal affairs.

ment to work with, so the U.S. government systematically began to change tribal governments into governments that closely resembled democratic structures. This movement went faster after individual tribal members were granted U.S. citizenship and voting rights.

In 1934, the United States required tribes to *incorporate* with the federal government under the provisions of the Indian Reorganization Act in order to be "recognized" as legitimate tribal nations. This act required tribes to have a *constitution* that resembled the U.S. or state constitutions. These tribal constitutions had to be approved by the Secretary of the Interior. These early constitutions are generally the ones under which tribal governments work today. These constitutions, like their state or federal counterparts, describe the powers and terms of office, as well as other intricacies of specialized government.

Today, tribal governments are representative democracies whereby individuals vote for members of the tribal council (governing body). The tribal council may or may not elect their own officers (tribal chairperson, vice chairperson) or those gaining the largest portion of votes in the tribal election may earn the executive offices. The constitutions of each tribe

The inside of the Sault tribe office building is a comfortable, modern environment, incorporating traditional motifs.

Indian tribes have the legal right to govern their lands and people who reside on those lands. This is the judicial building for the Sault St. Marie Band of Chippewa Indians.

vary and the specifics of governance vary, too. In general though, the tribal governments of the diverse Ojibwa communities are similar to the centralized governments that run states and counties.

Indian reservations are not "officially" a part of the states in which they reside. Rather, they are lands that the federal government holds in trust for specific groups of native people. This is an important point, since many people are confused over the status and jurisdiction of Indian tribes. Ojibwa tribes that have been federally recognized as legitimate tribal governments (usually **signatories** to historic Indian treaties) have a legal right to govern their lands and the people who reside there. Of course, federal law takes **precedence** over state or tribal law, but Indian tribes have the authority to pass and enforce laws.

There are some major exceptions, however. Back in 1885, the U.S. Congress passed the Major Crimes Act, which applied to Indian reservations across the land. Keep in mind that federal courts determined that Congress had absolute power over Indian affairs. With the passage of the Major Crimes Act, the U.S. government declared that the seven major crimes

The Chi Mukwa Community Recreation Center of the Sault St. Marie Chippewa tribe provides opportunities for indoor basketball, tennis, hockey, yoga, and a variety of activities for young and old. It is one example of how tribal money can be invested for the benefit of the whole community.

(murder, manslaughter, rape, assault with intent to kill, arson, burglary, and larceny) would be under the jurisdiction of the federal courts. Of course, this further weakened tribal governments at that time, since it clearly weakened the power of existing tribal courts.

Indian reservations are **trust lands** over which the U.S. federal government exerts power and control, with some authority being reserved by tribal governments. The powers exercised by tribal authority, however, are only those that the U.S. government has approved either by court or congressional action. This relationship between tribal governments and the United States goes back to Supreme Court decisions of the early 1830s, when the removal of Eastern Indians to the West was a national debate. In the 1831 case, *Cherokee Nation v. Georgia*, the Supreme Court issued a decision ruling that the status of Indian tribes within the United States was that of a "domestic, dependent Nation." The powers that have been retained by contemporary Ojibwa tribal governments flowed from this early decision and the laws passed later by Congress. Over time, these court decisions and congressional acts continued to erode the power and authority of tribal governments.

Today, Ojibwa/Chippewa tribal governments have the responsibility for many *civil* and criminal infractions that occur within the borders of their reservations. They provide police protection and many other important governmental services to tribal members, very much like regional governments provide to citizens at large.

Tribal governments are divided into numerous departments and specialized areas. Most tribes have departments of education, family services, conservation, personnel, and many other areas, as well as tribal courts and public safety. Ojibwa/Chippewa tribal governments also support cultural studies and language programs to help preserve distinctive traditions and life-ways. Tribal governments today are engaged in the range of professional activities that help people make successful transitions to the future. Tribes employ community planners and managers, and they support economic development committees comprised of tribal members and other

These are the tribal offices of the Saginaw Chippewa Indian tribe of Michigan.

The Chippewa have their own fire department.

professional staff. Governance is a complex activity that takes a great deal of time and commitment from elected tribal officials.

In many instances, elected tribal officials also have other job responsibilities. They are not professional politicians, as are many of our elected state and national office holders. In some cases, the tribal chairman's position is a full-time paid position, and deservedly so, since it is an incredibly important and busy position. Generally, though, tribal council members are not compensated at full-time levels for serving like congressional representatives or state senators. The task of serving tribal communities responsibly is a very difficult and often thankless job.

As with any other government, issues and priorities facing tribal governments change and need to be studied and acted on. Tribal members have differing opinions on how best to deal with these issues and what course of action should be followed. This is an important point. Tribal communities, like all communities, are not **unanimous** in their actions or opinions. Just like America's political parties, the Democrats and Republicans, tribal **factions** are at odds with each other. Heated debates are common in Indian Country on issues ranging from resource management to the feasibility of economic development projects. Issues are debated and studied—but when push comes to shove, what matters is if there are enough votes to win a majority to move an issue ahead. However, since Ojibwa/Chippewa tribal communities are often smaller than other governmental units, it may be easier for an individual to be heard on a given issue.

Clearly, there have been enormous changes over the years in the ways that Ojibwa/Chippewa communities govern themselves. Many of these changes were insisted on or introduced by the federal government out of a desire to work with Indian governments that had been restructured to resemble the national government. Without question, the Anishinabe's people experience with the colonies in North America had numerous implications. Some of the most important were the changes that have taken place over the last two centuries in how Native peoples govern their own communities and the gradual disintegration of the power of tribal governments.

Jesuit missionaries of the Roman Catholic Church established missions among the Anishinabe in the 1600s. Saint Isaac Jogues Catholic Church serves the Sault tribe today.

Chapter 4

Contemporary Ojibwa/Chippewa Religion

Y ou may or may not be considered a religious person, but you have no doubt been part of sacred ceremonies at special times. Baptisms, weddings, and funerals are occasions when people participate in time-honored sacred traditions. Today, the Ojibwa have many spiritual traditions, such as the practices of the Midewiwin Society, that began in the ancient past.

The word religion comes from the Latin term *religio*, which means to bond with God. So religion refers to the ways people in communities form bonds with God through common beliefs, common rituals, common dreams, common prayers, common stories, and common practices. Contemporary Ojibwa take part in a variety of religious and spiritual practices. Many Ojibwa, both on reservations and off, are Christians, belonging to any of a

Dale Thomas is pipe carrier, spiritual leader, and traditional teacher of the Sault tribe.

number of denominations. Many other Ojibwa follow **traditional** spiritual ways.

Some of the oldest Ojibwa/Chippewa stories tell of the bonds formed with the Great Spirit through the Midewiwin Society. As with many Ojibwa cultural practices, the midewiwin was a gift to the Anishinabe. The Great Spirit sent Nanaboozhoo to the people to teach them about healing medicines, to help carry them in times of sickness and need. The curing practices and beliefs of the midewiwin refer to a **mystical** tradition. According to that tradition, spirits protect and teach the Anishinabe through rites and the knowledge conveyed in ceremonies, dreams, and visions.

The Midewiwin Society is also known as the Grand Medicine Society. Some people say the term midewiwin comes from the combination of the words *mino*, meaning "good," and *daewaewin*, meaning "hearted." So the Midewiwin Society members might be viewed as the people of the good heart. Many of the teachings and records of the midewiwin are inscribed on birch bark scrolls.

To become part of the midewiwin, an Anishinabe must study with a midewiwin leader or priest. A candidate for the Midewiwin Society has gone through four orders, or degrees of instruction, to be **sanctioned** in the way of the midewiwin. Instruction involves mastery of a various bodies of knowledge. **Initiates** might be taught about plants and medicines, songs, prayers, and about the origins and the history of the Anishinabe. People of the midewiwin must also strive to live a life of integrity and good conduct. These aspects of their being and character were carefully reviewed and assessed by the leaders or medicine people of the midewiwin. Some midewiwin people go beyond four degrees, up to eight degrees of development of knowledge.

The Midewiwin Society is a very old spiritual tradition, but many contemporary Ojibwa still participate in the ceremonies and live their lives ac-

A fire is kept lit for someone who has died, a tradition kept alive at the Elijah Elk Cultural Center of the Saginaw Chippewa Indian tribe of Michigan.

Ojibwa artist Turtle Heart explains his painting titled Dream Style Singers: *"This is a drum painting. Before one may enter the 'house of dreamers,' a teaching lodge of the Ojibwa, the Bear clan has to be satisfied as to one's sincerity and correctness. The best way to do this is to make a song for the bear guardian. If the bear likes the song, then you get to go inside."*

cording to the teachings of the midewiwin. Although there are some minor differences in the midewiwin among different regions of the Anishinabe, the basics of the ceremonies are the same. The ceremonies or meetings of the midewiwin are usually held in the spring, and they usually last for several days. These ceremonies take place in a lodge specifically constructed for the meetings.

For many Ojibwa, the *pwaagun* or sacred pipe is also an important part of their ceremonial and spiritual life. The pipe was another gift to the people. (See chapter two.) Ojibwa/Chippewa people smoke the pipe in a variety of contexts. For example, people will often smoke the pipe before a feast, and sometimes they smoke the pipe before they begin a meeting. People also smoke the pwaagun during ceremonies. To this day, the pipe promotes peace and is used for prayer. Turtle Mountain Chippewa elder Francis Cree tells us that our thoughts are in the pipe when we smoke it—so we try to have good thoughts, for good purposes. Cree also says the pipe is like a telephone we can use to send those good thoughts to God and ask for help as long as we smoke with a good mind. As with all gifts from God, the pipe must be respected and cared for at all times.

Another important tradition for contemporary Ojibwa/Chippewa is the fasting ceremony. This ceremony is also known as a quest for a vision. Although this ceremony varies from region to region, the basics of the ceremony are similar.

Powwows are not sacred spiritual events, but they help to preserve ceremonial traditions.

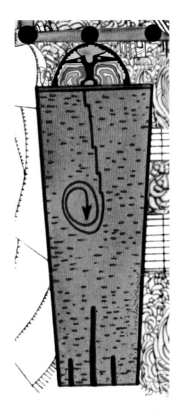

Ojibwa artist Turtle Heart explains his painting titled Birch Bark Man: *"To the Northern Forest tribal communities, birch bark remains an important and vital material. For centuries, teachings were preserved in birch bark by marking the inner bark, which is very resistant to decay. Homes, containers, tools, and treasures have come from the working of birch bark. A man may wrap himself in birch bark for many days as part of a lengthy teaching ceremony."*

Historically, when a boy was about twelve years old he would undertake a quest for a vision. He would go out alone into the woods or to a sacred place, where he would stay in a small, specially constructed lodge for a number of days without food and with little—in some cases, no—water. Through this process, the boy would pray and meditate with the hope of receiving a vision to guide him through his life, to give him purpose, and to help him serve his people.

Nowadays, Ojibwa still fast for a vision, but many people do so when they are older. Some people may undergo this quest to help them with particular problems or dilemmas they face. Other people may fast and seek a vision more than once. Some elders who help people prepare for the fasting ceremony require a certain number of days for the fast: some will say you must fast for four days, while others might say you should fast for two days. Still other teachers and teachings may ask the person seeking a vision to pledge a certain numbers of days for the fast. Basil Johnston writes in his book *Ojibwa Heritage:* "For some the vision came early, ending the quest and inaugurating a new phase of life, being. For others the vision came late." So some people have to fast for a long time to obtain a vision, and others may find their vision in fewer days of fasting.

Ojibwa/Chippewa tradition requires that a person go through a purification ceremony before fasting to seek a vision. This meant the person would go through a sweat lodge ceremony. For this ceremony, stones are heated in a fire. When the stones are red hot, they are brought into a small, dome-shaped frame lodge made of tree saplings. In the old days, the lodge was covered with animal skins or wide sections of tree bark. Today, the lodge might be covered with animal skins, bark, canvas, or blankets. The covering makes the lodge dark inside and it keeps in the heat. The door is a small opening in the lodge. When the hot stones are ready, all the people who are to participate in the ceremony enter through the door and sit in a circle. A bucket of water and a dipper, made from the leaves of a tree, are passed in through the door as well. Next, the hot stones are passed through the door and set into a circular hole dug in the earth, in the center of the lodge's interior. Two people inside the lodge use sticks to move the hot stones into the hole. The door is then covered. During the ceremony, the sweat leader prays and shakes water onto the stones. The water on the stones creates steam and heats up the lodge. The heat often becomes intense, and it makes the people sweat. The prayers, songs, and good thoughts of the people, in connection with the gift of the lodge as it was spiritually given, help to spiritually purify the people.

The sweat lodge ceremony is a fairly common spiritual practice among contemporary Ojibwa people, but as with other ceremonies, the lodges and the ceremonial process differ from area to area. In some lodges, for example, the leader will pass the bucket and the dipper to the next person on the left, and that person will pray and sprinkle the stones with water. In such a ceremony, each person will be given the opportunity to pray and offer water. In other cases, only one person, the leader, will pray and shake water onto the stones.

Churches like this one make visible the presence of Christianity among the Ojibwa/Chippewa people.

A number of contemporary Ojibwa also participate in the Big Drum ceremony. According to oral tradition, after a battle between Indians and whites, a young Sioux woman who was trapped in her village tried to flee. When she couldn't keep up with the others, she hid in a lake, where she was concealed by lily pads. The young woman hoped that the white men who were fighting her people would leave without seeing her, but they camped by the lake for six days. She went all that time without eating or drinking. In time a *manidoo*, or spirit, lifted her into the sky. The manidoo commended her for her courage and then gave her instructions on how to conduct the Dream Dance. The spirit also told her that the ceremony would help bring peace if she could convince her people to carry out the ceremony. The sacred drum was to be the center of the ceremony. The manidoo gave the young girl other instructions in the values associated with the drum ceremonies: the people of the Big Drum should strive for peace, act with responsibility, behave honorably, and be of service to others. The Sioux passed this ceremony on to the Ojibwa people in Minnesota. The ceremony spread throughout various communities in Minnesota and Wisconsin.

People who participate in the Big Drum ceremony have specific duties and roles. Those duties and roles refer to the origins of the ceremony, ceremonial spirit helpers, and the participants' relationship to the Great Spirit. For example, the leading women of the Big Drum ceremony represent Tailfeather woman, the young woman who brought the ceremony to the people.

Some people of the Plains Ojibwa/Chippewa also carry on a tradition known as the Thirsty Dance. In many ways this ceremony is similar to **Sun Dances** of other Plains tribes. At the same time, however, the Thirsty Dance has its own unique qualities, rituals, songs, and structure. This tradition was passed on to the Plains tribes a long time ago. According to Francis Cree, the ceremony originated in a place that is now known as Buffalo Lodge, North Dakota.

The ceremony runs for four days. During that time, dancers pledge to fast for a number of days. They go without food or water while dancing in place in a specially constructed circular **arbor**. The outer perimeter of the arbor consists of thirteen poles. From these thirteen poles, thirteen more poles are set as rafters that run from the perimeter poles to a tree in the interior. This is the sacred tree where people make offerings. A fire is kept near the tree inside the arbor, and an opening in the southern section of the arbor serves as the doorway. At the northern end of the arbor is an altar where pipes and sacred bundles are kept. The dancers are separated from the people by a railing. Near the northern part of the arbor, just inside the dancers' railing, a place is set aside for the drummers and singers. There are places inside the arbor for support people to sit and stand during the ceremony.

Some participants go through the ceremony to pray for sick relatives. Others seek help for personal or family problems. Still others may be seeking direction or a vision. Each dancer has a particular reason for dancing. Other people participate in the ceremony by drumming and singing. Still others support the dancers by being in the lodge and praying with the them.

While many contemporary Ojibwa follow traditional spiritual and religious ways, many others are involved in Christian religions. Every Ojibwa/Chippewa community has churches of various denominations. Some contemporary Ojibwa are Catholic, some are Methodist, some are Episcopalian, and some are Baptists.

George Ross grew up in the village of Naytahwaush on the White Earth Reservation in Minnesota. After retiring from his job as a supervisor for the

An outdoor fireplace for mourners.

Minneapolis Metro Transit System, he decided to study to be an Episcopal priest. After graduating from Seabury-Western Theological Seminary in Evanston, Illinois, George served as a priest on the White Earth Reservation for nine years. There he conducted services at St. Columba, in the village of White Earth, and at St. Philips, in the village of Rice Lake. After that, George served for four years as priest at St. Peter's Episcopal Church in Cass Lake, Minnesota. Now in his mid-seventies, George is formally retired, but he still participates in a variety of church activities and services in various reservation villages in northern Minnesota. As *testament* to his faith, George often travels to funerals and church gatherings to pray. He also supports church services by joining groups who sing hymns in the Ojibwa language.

During the *Lenten* season, George participates in celebratory feasts and services that alternate between different community churches on the Red Lake, the Leech Lake, and the White Earth Reservations. At these gatherings, people have a feast that begins at about five o'clock in the evening. After about ninety minutes, the service begins with a Christian hymn sung in Ojibwa. Then the people pray, sing again, and the priest reads from Scripture and comments on the reading. After another song, people at the service are welcome to speak individually. Then the people sing the "Lord's Prayer" in the Ojibwa language. After about three hours, the service ends with another hymn: "All Praise to Thee My Lord, God." Though George Ross knows of traditional Ojibwa ceremonies, and though he is a fluent speaker of the language, like a great many Ojibwa people he has dedicated his life—his being—to the ways of the Christian church.

Although George has chosen Christianity, George reflects the Ojibwa tradition that binds us to a community. This involves dedication to a way of being in the world, just as the people of the midewiwin, the Big Drum, and the Thirsty Dance are dedicated to lasting traditions. The same spirit also lives in people and ceremonies as they dedicate themselves to prayer, to honoring creation, to good thoughts, to service, and to the love and survival of community.

A powwow is an opportunity for celebration and renewal.

Chapter 5

Social Structures Today

Students at the Bahweting Anishinabe Public School Academy do many of the same things their peers across America do. They dress in jeans and T-shirts. They study math, science, and other subjects common to American and Canadian education. The school library has computers and model dinosaurs. But the Bahweting School also teaches many things that other schools do not. All subjects are taught with an emphasis on Anishinabe culture, language, and traditions. Students learn traditional tribal arts and crafts. This school is one place helping today's Ojibwa/Chippewa students keep and strengthen the social structures of their unique culture.

Ojibwa communities today have many different types of social structures. Social structures are those parts of society that facilitate or allow people to come together for shared purposes. They can occur naturally, like families, or they can be organized and administered by common agree-

Lou Ann Bush is a youth activities coordinator and traditional teacher. People like Lou Ann are increasingly important in strengthening and revitalizing Anishinabe culture among young people. She works for the Youth Education Action Program at the Chi Mukwa Community Recreation Center of the Sault St. Marie Chippewa tribe.

ment. Schools could be considered an important part of the social structure, as could recreational programs. The social structures of a community really define the social environment and opportunities within the community. If social structures are lacking, the social environment would be somewhat barren.

The social structure of a society can also be discussed in terms of how a society is organized and how it works. As an example, consider the idea of social class. Is social class and privilege an important or noticeable part of community life? If there is little emphasis on social class, how do people relate to each other? Historically, Ojibwa communities have not been class oriented; rather they have placed a great deal of importance on equality. Knowing this tells us a great deal about how people would be expected to behave and relate to other people within their community. It also tells us a great deal about what people value and how group interactions are structured.

One of the very basic, but incredibly important, social structures for Ojibwa communities is the family. Through the family, most cultural information and identity has been passed from one generation to the next. In the past and for those that still follow the tradition, Ojibwa children were born into the clan of their father. These super-families (named after animals) were a primary identity for young children as they grew up. They learned the characteristics of their animal ancestor (clan) and the traits for which they were known.

One of the original clans among the Ojibwa was the Crane Clan. They were known for their ability to see ahead and to speak to issues eloquently. Others revered them for their wisdom and role in civil leadership, but they were also known as capable warriors when needed.

At the Bahweting Anishinabe Public School Academy all subjects are taught with an emphasis on Anishinabe culture, language, and traditions.

The Big Bear Arena of the Sault tribe affords many opportunities for Sault tribal members to stay physically and emotionally fit.

Through the family, Ojibwa children came to understand their role in the context of the larger community of relatives. They also learned their obligations to their relatives at the same time. Of course, this very basic social structure was changed by the introduction of new ideas into Ojibwa/Chippewa communities. Colonial governments introduced and supported priests to work among the Ojibwa villages. The intent was to convert the "savages" (they were non-Christians) to Catholicism and to remake them in the image of Western Europeans. This long-term process is sometimes called **assimilation**; it changed traditional social structures, especially the family.

The U.S. government played a major role in attempting to reshape the Ojibwa family. In the nineteenth century, children were enrolled in manual labor training schools, where they were punished for speaking their native languages. The children were not allowed to return home for a long time. These policies were intended to weaken Chippewa families and culture.

Clearly, the policies of the federal government have worked to some degree. Today's Ojibwa social structures reflect traditional elements as well as Western ideas and practices. In some communities, the church is an extremely important social structure, and many of the Northern Ojibwa are

Catholics or Methodists. U.S. government policy forced Indians to do things as non-Indian society did them. The introduction of modern business, large-scale agriculture, and logging all helped to change the historic social structures of Ojibwa societies. Consequently, many reservations today really don't look very different from the surrounding communities. Nonetheless, both modern and traditional ways of doing things have persisted. This has broadened the range of social structures that are present in Ojibwa/Chippewa communities.

Children and young people can still learn about their heritage and culture. They can learn to fancy dance or shawl dance, and they can practice speaking their language or learn about tribal leaders in their schools. Young Ojibwa can do all of these things while still learning American history or algebra and preparing for jobs as engineers or computer programmers.

It is very important to Ojibwa/Chippewa tribes to *perpetuate* their distinct identity as Anishinabe (the original people). The family and larger community play an important role in shaping that identity through the opportunities that are provided to young people through schools and recreational programs.

Tribal colleges are a growing social structure that has arisen in Ojibwa/Chippewa communities. Numerous Ojibwa reservations now have tribal

Today's Ojibwa/Chippewa Indians live in modern housing, like these Sault tribe homes.

The powwow in its entirety is a colorful celebration of survival and reinvention, cultural heritage, and the future.

colleges that provide a community-based site for higher education. These colleges are very much like the community colleges that one would find elsewhere in the United States. They play an important role for both young people and adult learners who seek to continue their education or prepare themselves for new jobs in expanding tribal economies. The tribal colleges also provide a social setting to reward educational excellence and to host community events and programs. Parents are learning in the same environment as their children, and this clearly strengthens the bonds of both family and community.

Community celebrations are also an important part of the social structure of Ojibwa/Chippewa reservations. One of the most important events is the annual powwow. Most Ojibwa communities host a powwow, and the event is a celebration of continuation and renewal. In the context of the powwow, births will be celebrated, veterans and elders will be honored, and everyone will catch up on local news. Athletic dancers will be showcased, and singers will be praised for their years of hard work in mastering the old and new songs. The modern powwow has humorous times as well as more serious moments where honor songs will be sung for departed relatives, and the as-

Tribal Health and Human Services Center provides services to the Sault tribe.

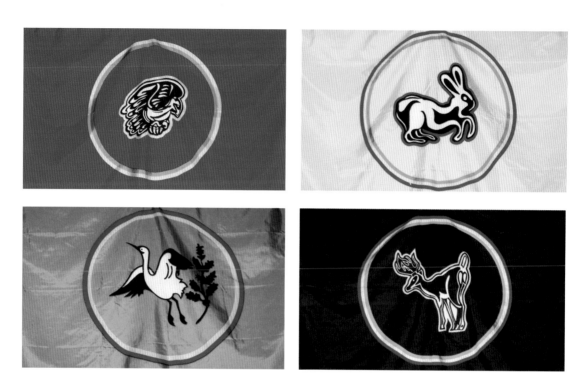

Flags representing various clans.

sembled people will share their grief. In its entirety, the powwow is a colorful celebration of survival and reinvention, cultural heritage, and the future.

The social structure of Ojibwa/Chippewa reservations is contained in three things: family, relatives, and community. Tribal institutions are built by cooperation between extended families. Large families who cooperate with other families to make policy and change the course of government significantly influence tribal politics.

Cooperation is an old and well-established value in Ojibwa communities. People may not agree all the time, and change may be difficult and sometimes divisive, but in the end, some form of agreement emerges. *Consensus* is reached through discussion and argument, leadership, and the wisdom of elders. This has been the path of decision-making in Chippewa villages for a long, long time.

An old prophesy is told among the Ojibwa that charges the people when making decisions to take into account the effect of their actions on the seventh generation, the generation yet unborn. Most people are aware of this wise, old saying, and some try to abide by it throughout their life. They consider the impact of their actions on the future and on the survival of the Anishinabe people as a whole.

Like all people, the Ojibwa are not perfect. As they strive to adjust to ongoing changes in a sometimes-hectic world, they make mistakes—but they also experience great successes. On some occasions, they fall prey to personal folly and take themselves too seriously. When that happens, their family and relatives guide them back to reality. This sense of responsibility to each other is the very core of Ojibwa life. It is what ensures each person the opportunity to fulfill his or her purpose in life—and it is the structure that knits together the society as a whole.

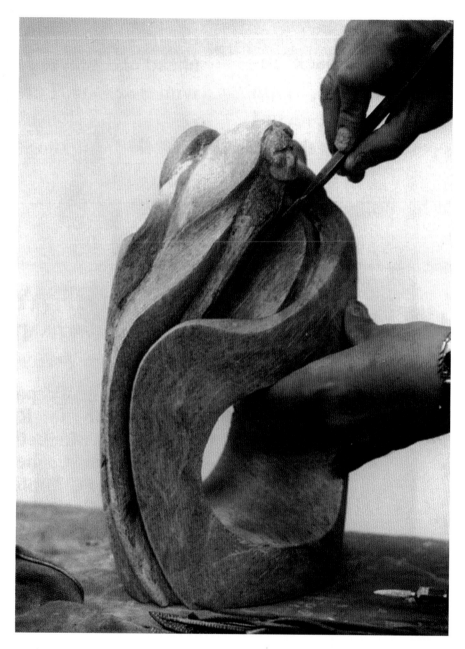

"When I first start out, I get a rock which comes from Mother Earth and looks like this, rough and jagged. But there's something in the stone I can feel. I can put my hands on it and rub it, and get the feel of the energy of the stone. It goes up my arms and into my heart." Daniel Mena Jr. describes the process of creating his stone sculptures in Mt. Pleasant Magazine.

Chapter 6

Ojibwa/Chippewa Arts

In September 2002, Francis and Rose Cree, of the Turtle Mountain Chippewa Tribe were flown to Washington, D.C., where they received one of America's highest honors for artistic work—a traditional arts lifetime achievement award and a National Heritage Fellowship—from the National Endowment for the Arts. Rose's honor was given for her traditional red willow basket work, and Francis was honored for his work as a storyteller and pipemaker. As is the case with many Native artists, the Crees' knowledge of traditional arts was passed on through their family, from generation to generation.

Francis and Rose are both over eighty years old. They have been married to each other for sixty-four years. They have had a long and rich life together.

From the time she was a young girl, Rose Cree worked alongside her mother to create baskets from red willow. In the process, Rose learned how to frame, shape, and weave baskets. At the same time, she was taught how to show proper respect for the red willow by offering tobacco each

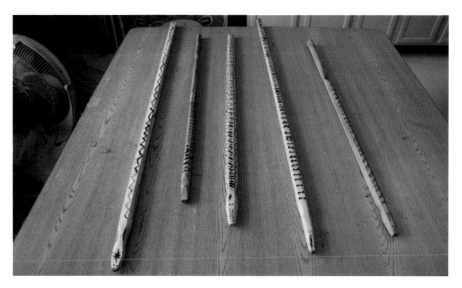

Snow Snakes are a traditional Anishinabe winter sport. The "snakes" are thrown underhand onto a snow trough. Players compete for the longest distance. Art students at the Bahweting Anishinabe Public School Academy made these snow snakes.

time she harvested materials. Rose also learned where and how to gather materials, ash for the frame and red willow for the weave, for the baskets. She learned that the materials for the baskets could only be gathered at certain times of the year. If the red willow were harvested when it was too dry, for example, it wouldn't be flexible enough to weave. After all the materials were gathered and properly prepared, Rose learned how to make baskets in a variety of shapes, sizes, and weave patterns, some in the shapes of animals, some with lids and handles. Now another generation of Crees has picked up red willow basketmaking from Rose. Her daughters, Debbie, Connie, and Brenda, all make red willow baskets.

Rose's husband, Francis, is well known throughout North Dakota, South Dakota, Montana, and Minnesota as a spiritual leader and a storyteller. In 2000, Francis received a Native American Music Award (NAMMY) for a recording titled *The Elders Speak*. The recording includes traditional stories by Francis and a Lakota elder, Mary Louise Defender Wilson. Like his wife, Francis learned his vocation from a very young age, as he was growing up on Turtle Mountain. His father, Charlie Cree, was a respected spiritual leader, and Francis learned many traditional ceremonies, songs, and stories from him. Francis's uncles and the elders in his community of Dunseith also taught him stories, ceremonies, and pipemaking.

Rose and Francis have traveled extensively throughout the United States to offer basketmaking workshops and to participate in storytelling festivals. Francis and Rose have also offered basketmaking and culture classes to children and adults in local Ojibwa schools in Dunsieth and Belcourt, North Dakota.

According to Ojibwa traditional teaching, each human being has gifts. To maintain the circle of creation and to overcome our shortcomings, we must share our human gifts and pass on the knowledge we have received. In the old days, if young Anishinabe men or women wanted to learn how to do something or develop particular skills or knowledge, they would go to an elder in their community and request help. Often the request would include a gift to the elder, such as a tobacco offering. If the elder accepted the offering, he or she would teach the young people until they became proficient in the particular skill or knowledge the elder shared with them. In almost all cases, it took many years for a person to learn what the elder

Reed shoes are another traditional craft learned by students at the Bahweting Academy.

Ojibwa artist Bear Heart calls this piece Bear Doctor. *The style of this painting is similar to that of famous Ojibwa artist Norval Morriseau.*

taught; it might even take a lifetime to become proficient in the area of knowledge passed on by an elder. In other instances, certain gifts, skills, and knowledge were passed on within families, from generation to generation. For example, if a father was a healer or a medicine person, he might pass on his knowledge to the son. If a mother was an artist, she might in turn teach her knowledge to her daughter or niece.

Anna Crampton of the Saginaw Chippewa Tribe, in Mt. Pleasant, Michigan, is also a traditional basket maker. Anna makes baskets from the black ash tree, an art that has been common among the Ojibwa/Chippewa for generations. A number of traditional artists in Michigan, Minnesota, Wisconsin, and Canada continue to make these baskets.

Like most traditional artists, Anna Crampton had to learn how to identify, harvest, and process natural materials to make her baskets. That included cutting a length of the ash and "pounding" the tree, so the bark could be loosened and peeled off in strips. Those strips would be used later to weave the baskets. Some black ash basket makers also dye strips of the barks to create colored patterns in the weave of the baskets. Anna learned under the direction of her mother from the time she was a young girl. Her son, Marclay Crampton, now makes black ash baskets as well, so that art form has been passed yet to another generation.

Another important traditional art among the Ojibwa involves birch bark basketry. Traditional birch bark basket makers harvest the outer bark from white birch and then stitch patterned pieces of the bark together with sinew, thin strands of willow, or natural twines made from basswood or cedar trees. Basket makers may also use pitch from spruce trees to hold baskets together at the folds. Many of the birch bark basket makers add

Daniel Mena Jr. works at his studio in the Saginaw Chippewa Indian tribe of Michigan's Seventh Generation Elijah Elk Cultural Center. He says he allows the stone to "dictate to me what it wants to be."

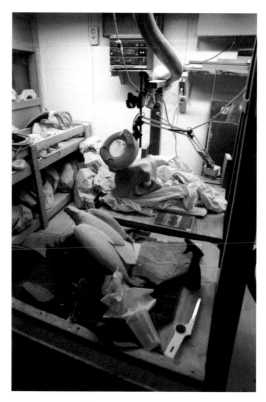

The stone sculpting artists studio at the Elijah Elk Cultural Center in Mt. Pleasant, Michigan.

porcupine quillwork, or sweetgrass to the outsides of baskets, along the top rim of basket openings or along the edges of basket lids.

In the past, these types of baskets were made for specific purposes. For example, some birch bark containers were made for food transportation, preparation, or storage. Today, birch bark baskets are made as decorative gift items as well as for utility. You will find birch bark basket makers in almost every contemporary Ojibwa/Chippewa community.

Beadwork is also an important traditional art among the Ojibwa. Unlike the geometric designs of other tribal groups, traditional Ojibwa beadwork is distinctive for its floral patterns. You will find examples of such beadwork on traditional clothing, including vests, jackets, moccasins, legging, shawls, pendants, and breechcloths, as well as on other personal items such as medicine bags. Contemporary Ojibwa beadworkers have expanded

Traditional Ojibwa decorative art.

the applications of beadwork to include the decorative art on a variety of things, from powwow *regalia*, to baseball caps, to checkbook covers, to earrings, to hairclips.

Many modern Ojibwa/Chippewa artists work in other *media* with materials common to European-American artistic traditions. Ojibwa artists include painters, colored pencil-and-ink artists, sculptors, photographers, writers, singers, dancers, and actors. While many of these artists are working in media of the larger culture, their work often reflects traditional Anishinabe themes, values, and *motifs*. Some Ojibwa art addresses issues related to their identity as Anishinabe in particular, or as an American Indian in general.

Frank Big Bear is an example of an Ojibwa artist who creates contemporary art. He was born in 1953 on the White Earth Reservation in Minnesota. Later, Frank moved to Minneapolis, where he spent most of his life among the urban Indian community there. He has been drawing since he was a child, but he received little training in art. Like many traditional artists, Frank worked with an elder to develop his skill and knowledge. He cites Ojibwa artist George Morrison as an artistic influence, as well as a *mentor* who taught him how to live as an Anishinabe. Frank worked with Morrison in a Studio Arts Program at the University of Minnesota for about a year.

Today, Frank Big Bear works mostly with Prisma color pencils. He prefers them over oils and acrylics because they offer more immediate effects and are compatible with his particular artistic style and process. According to Jacki Thompson Rand, a history professor at the University of Iowa:

> Frank's drawings reflect personal experiences and impressions drawn from growing up in the city as a member of a generation of young men and women who, through political action and artistic expression, gave voice to a critique of the history of contact in America. Although Big Bear's work exhibits a rejection of "traditional" representations of Native America, it is clearly situated in his ties to and membership in the Chippewa community.
>
> Over time, the content of his work has spanned a range of themes. His earliest pieces are intensely personal and reflect a strong preoccupation with Indian male identity. Later works broaden to themes of more general social and political commentary and reflections on the history of Indian-Anglo relations. In recent years, Frank has embraced post-modern

representations of "traditional" themes, particularly in the area of warrior images.

Frank also worked as an Artist in Residence at the Heart of the Earth Survival School in Minneapolis in 1973. From 1994 through 1998, he worked on a mural project for P.S. 75, Brooklyn's Mayda Cortiella School. The New York City Percent for Art Program commissioned the work, and the mural, titled *Dream Catcher Love Song*, was installed in 1998.

Over the years, more than twenty solo exhibitions have been dedicated to Frank Big Bear's work. He has also received four arts fellowships to continue his work. Two of his fellowships were from the Bush Foundation, one was from the McKnight Foundation, and one was from the Jerome Foundation.

Frank Big Bear's mentor George Morrison (1919–2000), a Minnesota

Stone carvings reflect Ojibwa creativity.

Dream Catchers

Dream catchers are very popular items today. You see them hanging in many people's homes, and Indians and non-Indians make and sell them. This popular tradition actually began with the Chippewa/Ojibwa. According to tradition, Asibikaasi (Spider Woman) took care of all the Anishinabe. When the Ojibwa Nation migrated, Asibikaashi had a difficult time making her journey to all the people. So mothers took up the practice of weaving these magical webs from willow hoops and sinew for their new babies in the shape of a circle to represent the sky. The dream catcher filtered out all the bad *bawedjigewin* (dreams).

It was traditional to put a feather in the center of the dream catcher. An owl's feather represented wisdom, and the eagle feather stood for courage. Since owl and eagle feathers are sacred and cannot be sold, many modern dream catchers substitute four beads, representing the four sacred directions, instead. Most dream catchers have seven or eight points where the sinew connects with the hoop: seven for the seven fires, or eight for the spider's legs.

Ojibwa, was also highly respected for his work. For many years, Morrison worked with a group of **abstract expressionist** painters in New York, and through that experience he developed a unique vision. Morrison also branched out from painting to work with sculpture and **collage**.

Another of the most influential and noted Ojibwa artists is Norval Morriseau, Copper Thunderbird. Morriseau is a Canadian Ojibwa from the Sand Point Reserve in Ontario. He is considered one of the founders of a woodland style of art that is also known as legend or medicine painting. This type of art refers back to traditional legends for influences and often depicts natural scenes. In many cases, these natural scenes are considered "X-ray art," because they show a natural form, such as an animal or a plant, inside a larger natural form. Morriseau's style of painting and his use of traditional motifs influenced a number of Canadian Ojibwa artists, including Francis Kagige and Daphne Odjig.

Frank Big Bear, Norval Morriseau, and George Morrison are just a few of the many Ojibwa artists whose artistic achievement has been recognized regionally and nationally. David Bradley, White Earth Anishinabe, is another

The Ojibwa/Chippewa are good woodworkers.

highly regarded painter. Painter Daniel Ramirez and sculptor Daniel "Gomez" Mena of the Saginaw Chippewa Tribe of Michigan are also producing excellent work in their particular media. Frank Big Bear's son, Star Wallowing Bull, is also an artist. His work shows great imagination and a wide-ranging vision.

There are literally hundreds of Ojibwa/Chippewa artists throughout Canada and the U.S. Midwest. They are transforming artistic expression while tapping into their Ojibwa roots for inspiration and meaning. Many are forging a unique vision that often reflects with passion and humor on the ironies and inconsistencies in relationship between American Indians and the larger communities in which they interact and live.

The Seventh Generation Program on the Saginaw Chippewa Reservation has a greenhouse where they grow herbs and traditional medicines such as tobacco, sweetgrass, sage, mint, and ginseng.

Chapter 7

Contributions to the World

In the book *Ojibwa Heritage*, Basil Johnston, a Canadian Ojibwa, tells how the Great Spirit beheld a vision and then created the world according to that vision. For both Anishinabe of the past and the present, it is important for human beings to have a vision to guide and lead them. Through our visions we can establish a purpose and set goals as we try to bring that vision into the world. Many contemporary Ojibwa/Chippewa people have been inspired by their vision to create new possibilities for their people.

Winona LaDuke, for example, is a Mississippi Band, White Earth Anishinabe, of the Mukwa Dodem, or Bear Clan. She was born in 1959 and spent most of her early life in Los Angeles, California. Her father, Vincent LaDuke, was an actor who played supporting parts in Hollywood westerns. He was also an Indian *activist*. Her mother Betty was an artist and college professor. A 1982 graduate of Harvard University, Winona became active in American Indian environmental issues while attending school

Milton Pelcher is director of the Saginaw Chippewa Seventh Generation Program, which works to preserve the language and culture of the tribe. Pelcher and the Seventh Generation team offer weekly tobacco and sweat lodge ceremonies, monthly basketmaking workshops, youth workshops for the local tribal school, and community feasts.

there. Since then, she has established herself as a major voice for American Indian environmental and political rights. She has spoken before the United Nations on American Indian issues, and she has been instrumental in establishing a number of organizations for American Indian rights. In 1989, Winona received a Reebok International Human Rights Award for her work on environmental issues and American Indian rights. She serves as co-chair for the Indigenous Women's Network, a North American and Pacific **indigenous** women's organization. She is also the program director for the Honor the Earth Fund, and has served as program director of the environmental program for the Seventh Generation Fund. In 1994, *Time* magazine named Winona one of America's fifty most promising leaders under the age of forty. In 1995, she spoke on behalf of American Indian people at the United Nations Fourth World Congress on Women, and in 1998, *Ms.* magazine named Winona Woman of the Year for her work with Honor the Earth. She has also been involved in national and international environmental movements, and she formerly served as a board member for Greenpeace USA.

After graduating from Harvard, Winona settled on the White Earth Reservation. There she became involved with Anishinabe Akeeng, a local land rights organization at White Earth. Winona and the group worked to recover tribal land that had been illegally taken from White Earth tribal members. Anishinabe Akeeng did exhaustive legal research into tribal land loss on the reservation. They also initiated legal efforts to regain land that had been stolen by the federal, state, and county governments. As part of the legal effort, Winona, Dale Hanks, Marvin Manypenny Richard, Raymond Bellecourt, John Morrin, and other members of Anishinabe Akeeng interviewed White Earth tribal members to get *depositions* and information to initiate lawsuits on behalf of the people. They also organized protests and marches to create public awareness of White Earth Land issues.

When all legal options were exhausted, Winona founded the White Earth Land Recovery Project (WELP) with funds she received from her Reebok Human Rights Award. The primary focus of WELP is to raise funds to buy back lands originally held by White Earth people. The organization hopes to regain enough land to sustain traditional harvesters and crafts-people, and to provide sources of traditional medicines from plants and herbs. Further, WELP would like to get land to meet some of the agriculture

The Seventh Generation Program on the Saginaw Chippewa Reservation in Mt. Pleasant, Michigan, strives to provide the Saginaw Chippewa tribal community with programs and activities that connect them to Anishinabe spiritual traditions.

Ojibwa Artist Turtle Heart titled this painting Seven Generations. *He describes its meaning: "The cultural leadership of the tribal family often reminds us that we stand between the seven generations behind us and the seven generations before us. The consequences of our collective behavior reach far ahead of us. Among the Ojibwa and other tribes, Turtle is the symbol of this Mother Earth."*

needs of the White Earth people. Their efforts to reacquire land are motivated by a deep-seated **ethic** that requires responsible stewardship of the environment. They are concerned for the physical and spiritual dimensions of all these resources.

Under Winona's leadership, with the efforts of dozens of talented Ojibwa, the White Earth Land Recovery Project has evolved into a multifaceted organization committed to the cultural traditions of the Anishinabe. WELP work encompasses sustainable energy programs, which includes implementation of a pilot project using both solar and wind energy. As part of that effort, WELP purchased a wind generator as an alternative source for electricity for tribal facilities. WELP also has plans to install solar panels to provide power for land recovery offices and facilities. The White Earth Land Recovery Project also maintains a catalog sales business called Native Harvest. Through Native Harvest, people can purchase foods Anishinabe people have traditionally gathered and produced for hundreds of years, such as wild rice, *hominy*, raspberry products, organic coffee, and maple syrup. In addition, Native Harvest supports the work of traditional artists and crafts people by offering birch bark baskets, beadwork, and quilts for sale through the catalog business. Many of those traditional artists are supported through the WELP Niijii Development fund as well. Other White Land Recovery Project initiatives include a forest maintenance and management program, a food for elders program, an effort to protect the genetic integrity of traditional wild rice species through *patents*, and a program to reintroduce sturgeon into White Earth natural water systems.

The White Earth Land Recovery Project also has an educational component that embraces key concerns as well. An important aspect of this component is preserving Anishinabemowin, the language of the Ojibwa/Chippewa people. Under this program, WELP has worked with public and tribal schools and with language speakers from the University of Minnesota to develop school programs and *language immersion* camps. Combating racism is also part of WELP's educational efforts. A number of White Earth youth have gone through training to serve as leaders under this initiative. WELP has also set up a young women's leadership program. One part of this program, the Niiganikwe Girls Club, connects girls ages ten to eighteen with tribal elders, so the girls can learn about Anishinabe culture and develop understanding while they foster relationships with community role models. For another part of the young women's program, WELP worked with Women's Rights International to bring in Dr. Shana Swiss to educate people about violence against women. This program also brought young Ojibwa girls from urban areas to the reservation to meet with and learn from reservation women.

The Seventh Generation Program on the Saginaw Chippewa Reservation in Mt. Pleasant is dedicated to many of the same cultural concerns as the White Earth Land Recovery Project. Seventh Generation strives to provide the Saginaw Chippewa Tribal community with programs and activities that connect them to Anishinabe spiritual traditions. Director Milton Beaver Pelcher supervises a team that includes assistant director Raul Vanegas, two administrative assistants, four cultural coordinators, a home economist, a youth worker, a maintenance person, a stone sculpture instructor, and a woodshop instructor. The program teaches the correct way to use sacred objects and medicines and the proper access to ceremonies. According to the Seventh Generation Web site, this is done with the intention of establishing a "closer relationship to the Great Spirit through hands-on individual and community spiritual development."

The Saginaw Chippewa, Seventh Generation Program also hopes to maintain and preserve the culture and language of the tribe. Pelcher and the Seventh Generation team offer weekly tobacco and sweat lodge ceremonies, monthly basketmaking workshops, youth workshops for the local tribal school, and seasonal community feasts. Each spring the program sets up a community camp for harvesting and processing maple syrup.

Seventh Generation also works to develop better relationships between people and the environment. It has a community garden in which all food is organically grown, without chemicals or pesticides. The program maintains a community greenhouse where they grow herbs and traditional medicines such as tobacco, sweetgrass, sage, mint, and ginseng. The garden and greenhouse also help to educate community youth as they participate in planting, crop care, and harvesting during each growing cycle.

Through Seventh Generation, Saginaw Chippewa tribal members and local community members may receive instruction in stone sculpture and woodworking. The Seventh Generation Program maintains a well-equipped workshop for both these activities.

Feasts, seasonal events, and ceremonies take place in the Seventh Generation ceremonial house, and Seventh Generation staff and volunteers prepare meals for community activities in a community kitchen. A tribal women's group often uses the kitchen for meetings as well.

The vision behind organizations like the White Earth Land Recovery Project and the Saginaw Chippewa Seventh Generation Program may be found in the term "seventh generation." What we do today, how we treat others, how we treat all our relations—human, animal, plant, mineral—physically, emotionally, mentally, spiritually, all will have effects on seven generations to come. As Anishinabe, as Native people, as human beings, we should also consider this wisdom as we seek a vision, as we fulfill our purpose, as we give thanks on this good earth.

Today, more than 50 percent of all American Indian people live off reservations; many American Indian people live in urban areas. This is true of the Ojibwa/Chippewa as well. Urban areas such as Chicago, Detroit, Minneapolis-St. Paul, Grand Rapids, Michigan, and Duluth all have substantial Ojibwa populations. In fact, Anishinabe people are spread all over the United States. While they live and work in urban areas, they maintain a connection to their tribal heritage.

Many Ojibwa/Chippewa are also professionals with extensive education. Paulette F. Molin, has a doctorate in educational administration. A member of the Minnesota Chippewa Tribe from White Earth Reservation, she has worked in the field of education for many years. Her professional experiences include work in educational programs of the Minneapolis public schools, including serving as director of an Indian elementary curriculum project. This project provided classroom instruction, curriculum development, and other educational services to students, parents, and teachers in a number of schools. In Virginia, Molin served as Assistant Dean of the Graduate College and Director of the American Indian Educational Opportunities Program at Hampton University. While there, she co-curated the photographic exhibition, *To Lead and to Serve: American Indian Education at Hampton Institute, 1878 to 1923*. Molin is also the author of several publications about early students at Hampton. She is the co-curator of the permanent exhibition, *Enduring Legacy: Native Peoples, Native Arts at Hampton*, which opened in the American Indian gallery of the Hampton University Museum in 1999.

Molin currently devotes her efforts to writing projects. She is the coeditor of *American Indian Stereotypes in the World of Children*, second edition, with Arlene Hirschfelder and Yvonne Wakim (Scarecrow Press, 1999). This publication received the Writer of the Year Award for prose (reference) from Wordcraft Circle of Native Writers and Storytellers in 1999. She is also the coauthor, with Arlene Hirschfelder, of *Encyclopedia of Native American Religions* (Facts On File, 1992, 2000, 2001), which was named New York Public Library Outstanding Reference Book in 1992. The updated edition was cited as a Book of the Month Club selection in 2002.

Many other contemporary Anishinabe who are living off reservations are making important cultural contributions as well. For example, Brenda Child McNamara, a Red Lake Anishinabe, is a history professor at the University of Minnesota. Jeannie O'Brien, a White Earth tribal member, directs the American Indian Studies Program at the University of Minnesota. Kimberly Blaeser, another White Earth Anishinabe, is also a college professor and a published writer. She teaches in the Department of Comparative Literature at the University of Wisconsin–Milwaukee. Kimberly's brother, Robert Blaeser, is a judge for the Minnesota juvenile court system. Terri Yellowhammer, who is both Anishinabe and Lakota, is a lawyer with the State of Minnesota Department of Social Services.

Clearly, the Ojibwa/Chippewa are making a difference to the world where they live.

Wilma Henry serves as a cultural representative at the Seventh Generation Elijah Elk Cultural Center in Mt. Pleasant, Michigan. The Seventh Generation Program works to ensure that the future of the Chippewa people will be guided by the spiritual wisdom of their traditions.

Chapter 8

Challenges for Today, Hopes for Tomorrow

Ojibwa/Chippewa tribal governments have endured a great deal over time. They have fought to retain their lands and access to natural resources. They've **litigated** in federal courts to protect their constitutionally guaranteed treaty rights and tribal sovereignty. They've survived epidemics, poverty, and having their children placed in government schools. Throughout all of these experiences, though, the Ojibwa have never lost sight of who they are and from where they came.

Without question, the last thirty years have witnessed many positive changes in Ojibwa/Chippewa communities. Self-determination, the ability to have a voice in what happens, is becoming a way of life for the Ojibwa. Reservations have won important court cases that have reaffirmed their rights to use natural resources for self-sufficiency and economic well-being. Tribal governments have also expanded human services to reservation

Since 1988, there has been enormous growth in both the size and complexity of tribal economies as casino interests have expanded. The Soaring Eagle Casino in Mt. Pleasant, Michigan, owned by the Saginaw Chippewa tribe, is one of the largest in the Midwest.

populations and created economic climates that provide jobs to Indians and non-Indians in the surrounding areas. These changes were accomplished by a devoted group of Ojibwa/Chippewa people who contested U.S. government action and set the stage for meaningful community development initiatives.

Probably the most important outcome of these actions was the creation of Chippewa gaming facilities throughout the Midwest. The first tribally owned and managed casino in Indian Country was established on the Bay Mills Indian Community reservation on Michigan's Upper Peninsula. The casinos developed out of bingo games that initially were run on a fairly small scale in most Chippewa communities. Many states, like Michigan, also licensed charitable organizations to hold "Las Vegas Nights," where it was legal to wager money in card games and other games of chance. This was deemed to be perfectly legal as long as the money the charitable organization won was used for social purposes. Chippewa Indian tribes began to replicate the activities that states licensed for charitable organizations with one important difference: the tribes claimed they were empowered to regulate their own games and the amount of money that anyone was allowed to wager or win. The states disagreed with this notion and threatened to close down the establishments. On more than one occasion, federal authorities also threatened legal action.

The difference of opinion between the tribes and the states was eventually settled in federal court and then was heard on appeal by the U.S. Supreme Court. In the now-famous case *California v. Cabezon* (1987), the Supreme Court decided in a majority decision that tribes could engage in

Seventh Generation produces maple syrup.

In the Big Bear Recreational Facility, Sault St. Marie, Michigan, hang three flags—Canadian, American, and tribal, representing the citizenships of today's Anishinabe people.

gaming practices that were not illegal in respective states. Since Michigan, as an example, allowed Las Vegas Nights where betting could occur, the court determined that it was perfectly legal for tribes to do the same. The regulatory power of the tribes to operate the gaming establishments was reaffirmed, and later, the U.S. Congress passed the Indian Gaming Regulatory Act (1988), which established the guidelines under which tribal casinos could operate. These actions, both judiciary and congressional, set the stage for prolonged economic growth on Chippewa reservations in the United States. Since 1988, there has been enormous growth in both the size and complexity of tribal economies as casinos have expanded.

This growth has clearly been a challenge to tribal governments and managers. It has also created new opportunities and much-needed employment and training options for tribal members and non-Indian citizens residing near reservations. Chippewa tribal governments are now some of the largest employers in the upper Midwest, and the economic ripple effects of successful tribal businesses are being experienced in many regions. The revenues from casino operations are playing an increasingly important role in funding much-needed tribal programs in the areas of education, social services, health, and cultural programs. Any effective government must have the means to fund programs that enhance the quality of life for its members, and most Ojibwa/Chippewa tribes are now funding higher education programs and scholarships for tribal members. This is a critical step in developing future leaders who possess the skills and knowledge necessary to manage tribal programs in the future.

The growth of Chippewa tribal casinos and revenues has drastically reduced unemployment on reservations and provided a new respectability for Indian governments. These same tribal governments are now seen as important players in regional economies and local and state politics. Most Chippewa tribal casinos also provide financial support to regional non-Indian government agencies (such as police and fire protection) as well as to service organizations that are near reservations. This has been the result of agreements between states and specific Chippewa tribes under the provisions of the Indian Gaming Regulatory Act. These contributions have assisted tribal governments in building stronger community relations with non-Indian citizens living near reservations.

Numerous challenges face Ojibwa governments in the area of government-to-government relations with local, state, and federal agencies. Agreements tied to treaty rights, like hunting and fishing, still need to be

Childcare centers help build the future for the Ojibwa/Chippewa people.

An artist's rendering of the future Sault tribe of Chippewa Indians' facilities.

improved and fine-tuned. Tribal governments continue to work to protect their sovereignty and ensure that their rights under treaty agreements are maintained for future generations. The U.S. government continues to pass legislation that impacts Indians nationally, and tribal officials must make sure that their voices are being heard on the issues being debated.

Even though the challenges facing Ojibwa/Chippewa tribal governments are complicated and numerous, the future is bright. The quality of life for most Ojibwa is much better than it was twenty or thirty years ago. People have more choices, and tribal governments are doing a much better job in providing services to their membership. Tribal governments are engaged in planning a future that few could have imagined three decades ago. Access to higher education has been an incredibly important part of the current state of affairs, and numerous young Ojibwa people are purposefully working to continue the trend of growth and expansion.

Chippewa tribal governments will work to acquire additional lands for tribal recreation and ceremonial purposes. These same governments will also be acquiring lands to guarantee access to and protect natural resources that are important to the cultural and ceremonial life of the

Anishinabe. People are working to strengthen that relationship and ensure that young people will have more opportunities in the coming years. One can expect to see more young Indian professionals in the fields of natural resource management and protection. All of these efforts and developments will prove to be critical as the Ojibwa move into the twenty-first century.

One can also expect to see tribal governments providing more funding and support to reinvigorate the cultural practices of the Anishinabe. Language preservation and instruction is a priority for many communities. Likewise, there is strong support for teaching young people about traditional practices. Tribal governments are also interested in teaching non-Indians about their history and culture. Many Chippewa governments support the growth of cultural institutions that have the mission of teaching others about tribal life and the numerous contributions that Indians have made to world civilization. These activities are important in building cultural understanding and correcting misconceptions about Indian people.

These tribal institutions will reinforce the idea and reality that the Anishinabe are still here—and they are here to stay. They are not artifacts of

The Sugar Island Cultural Camp is a weekend retreat center. It also provides storytelling and activities for children.

These Ojibwa/Chippewa children are a part of the twenty-first century.

The Ojibwa have always lived closely to the Earth.

The Ojibwa/Chippewa people are following their path to a strong future.

history or parts of museum displays. They are a living, prospering people who have survived and adapted to conflict and change.

Ojibwa/Chippewa people have the same hopes and aspirations for their children that most Americans hold dear. They want their children to have the opportunity to get a good education, and they want them to be happy and healthy. They want to see their children grow up in safe environments and engage in meaningful work that makes the world a somewhat better place. They want all this, and yet they still want their children to know that they are the descendents of once-great nations who still retain a cultural and political identity within the context of the United States.

When you look at the smiling faces of Anishinabe children, you can read the future. As these children grow and mature, and as their talents unfold, they will create an even better world for their children. Their dreams will become a world no one today can even imagine.

Further Reading

Beyer, David, and Johnston, Basil. *Ojibwa Ceremonies*. Lincoln: University of Nebraska Press, 1990.

Clifton, James, George Cornell, and James McClurken. *People of the Three Fires: The Ottawa, Potawatomi, and Ojibwa of Michigan*. Sault Sainte Marie, Mich: Michigan Indian Press, 1986.

Danziger, Edmund Jefferson. *The Chippewas of Lake Superior*. Norman: University of Oklahoma Press, 1990.

Graham, Loren R. *A Face in the Rock: The Tale of a Grand Island Chippewa*. Berkeley: University of California Press, 1998.

Henry, Gordon. *The Light People: A Novel*. Norman: University of Oklahoma Press, 1993.

For More Information

The Minnesota Chippewa Tribe
www.mnchippewatribe.org/

Ojibwa Culture and History
www.geocities.com/Athens/Acropolis/5579/ojibwa.html

Ojibwa Information
www.rootsweb.com/~minatam/ojibwa.html

Sagginaw Chippewa Indian Tribe
www.sagchip.org/

The Sault Sainte Marie Tribe of Chippewa Indians
www.sootribe.org/

Publisher's Note:

The Web sites listed on this page were active at the time of publication. The publisher is not responsible for Web sites that have changed their address or discontinued operation since the date of publication. The publisher will review and update the Web sites upon each reprint.

Glossary

abstract expressionist: An artist of the movement of the mid-twentieth century that emphasized the artist's ability to convey emotions through nonrepresentational forms.

activist: Someone who does things in support of a cause.

alienating: Causing to be withdrawn or diverted.

arbor: A lattice covered with vines or leaves.

assimilation: The process by which a group is blended into the culture of the majority of a population.

centralized: Concentrated power in a central organization.

cessions: Formal occasions of yielding or giving in to another.

civil: Relating to private rights and remedies sought by action or suit.

collage: An artwork created by the assembling of various materials glued onto a surface.

collective: A number of persons considered as a whole, rather that as individuals.

colonial: Relating to a colony, especially one of the original thirteen American colonies.

consensus: An agreement reached by most of those concerned.

constitution: The basic principles and laws of a nation, state, or social organization.

democratic process: The method of government in which the supreme power rests in the people, directly or indirectly, usually through a representative system.

depositions: Testimony under oath taken down in writing.

direct representation: The process by which the public elects the people who stand in for them in the government.

discrimination: Prejudicial outlook, action, or treatment based on certain characteristics, such as race or religion.

empire: A political authority having much territory.

epic: A long narrative poem telling the story of a legendary hero.

epidemic: An outbreak of a disease affecting a large number of people in a population or community.

ethic: A moral principle.

factions: Subgroups that often don't get along with each other.

hominy: Kernels of corn that have been soaked in a solution and then rinsed to remove the hulls.

immunity: Being able to resist a disease.

incorporate: To form a corporation.

indigenous: Having originated in a particular region.

initiates: Persons being instructed in the principles of something.

language immersion: A method of teaching a foreign language in which only the language being taught is used.

Lenten: Pertaining to the period of Lent, the forty weekdays between Ash Wednesday and Easter.

litigated: Carried on a judicial process.

media: Materials used to create art.

mentor: A trusted counselor or teacher.

motifs: A recurring idea or central theme.

mystical: Having to do with the spiritual world.

oratory: Public speaking.

paradigms: Patterns or models; ways of thinking about something.

patents: Legal documents providing the inventor the exclusive right to make, use, or sell an invention for a specified number of years.

perpetuate: To make to last indefinitely.

pictographs: Drawings or paintings on a rock wall.

precedence: Priority of importance.

regalia: The emblems and symbols of royalty.

reservations: Land put aside by the government for the use of American Indians.

sanctioned: Granted by formal decree.

signatories: Those who signed something.

sovereignty: Freedom from external control.

Sun Dances: A spiritual ceremony common to many American Indian groups.

testament: Tangible proof or tribute.

traditional: Having to do with a culture's inherited practices, beliefs, or customs.

trust lands: A non-self-governing territory placed under an administrative authority.

unanimous: Complete agreement.

vested: Granted a particular authority.

war industries: Businesses that supply the military with supplies.

Western: Having to do with the culture of the United States and Western Europe.

Index

Biographies

George Cornell, an Ojibwa tribal member, is professor of English and history and director of the Native American Institute at Michigan State University. He also serves on the Board of Trustees to the National Museum of the American Indian at the Smithsonian Institution. He is author of the nonfiction book *People of the Three Fires*.

Gordon Henry is an enrolled member of the Chippewa tribe at the White Earth Reservation. He studied at Michigan State University and earned his Ph.D. in Literature at the University of North Dakota. He has taught at Ferris State University in Big Rapids, Michigan, and at Michigan State University. He is the author of the novel *The Light People*.

Martha McCollough received her bachelor's and master's degrees in anthropology at the University of Alaska-Fairbanks, and she now teaches at the University of Nebraska. Her areas of study are contemporary Native American issues, ethnohistory, and the political and economic issues that surround encounters between North American Indians and Euroamericans.

Benjamin Stewart, a graduate of Alfred University, is a freelance photographer and graphic artist. He traveled across North America to take the photographs included in this series.